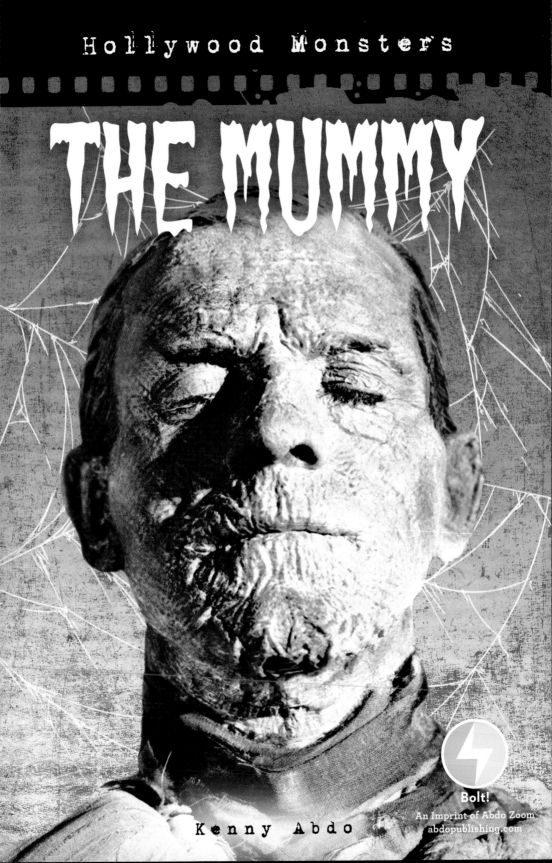

Hollywood Monsters

THE MUMMY

Kenny Abdo

Bolt!
An Imprint of Abdo Zoom
abdopublishing.com

abdopublishing.com

Published by Abdo Zoom, a division of ABDO, P.O. Box 398166, Minneapolis, Minnesota 55439. Copyright © 2019 by Abdo Consulting Group, Inc. International copyrights reserved in all countries. No part of this book may be reproduced in any form without written permission from the publisher. Bolt!™ is a trademark and logo of Abdo Zoom.

Printed in the United States of America, North Mankato, Minnesota.
052018
092018

THIS BOOK CONTAINS
RECYCLED MATERIALS

Photo Credits: Alamy, Everette Collection, Granger Collection, iStock, Shutterstock
Production Contributors: Kenny Abdo, Jennie Forsberg, Grace Hansen
Design Contributors: Dorothy Toth, Neil Klinepier

Library of Congress Control Number: 2017960602

Publisher's Cataloging-in-Publication Data

Names: Abdo, Kenny, author.
Title: The mummy / by Kenny Abdo.
Description: Minneapolis, Minnesota : Abdo Zoom, 2019. | Series: Hollywood monsters |
    Includes online resources and index.
Identifiers: ISBN 9781532123207 (lib.bdg.) | ISBN 9781532124181 (ebook) |
    ISBN 9781532124679 (Read-to-me ebook)
Subjects: LCSH: Monsters & myths--Juvenile literature. | Monsters in literature-
    Juvenile literature. | Monsters in mass media--Juvenile literature.
Classification: DDC 398.2454--dc23

TABLE OF CONTENTS

The Mummy 4

Origin 6

Hollywood 12

Legacy 18

Glossary 22

Online Resources 23

Index 24

THE MUMMY

The Mummy is about an old Egyptian named Imhotep. His **mummified** body is accidentally brought back to life by **archeologists**. Disguised as a modern Egyptian, the mummy searches for his lost love.

The Mummy has become
one of the most recognized
figures in horror history.

ORIGIN

The Mummy was based on real-life history. The story was inspired by the opening of King Tutankhamun's tomb in 1922.

It was also based on what is known as the curse of the pharaohs. It is believed that any person who disturbs a mummy will be cursed for life.

The name Imhotep was taken from an actual Egyptian. Imhotep was the **architect** who designed the **pyramids**. He was made a god after his death.

11

HOLLYWOOD

The Mummy, starring Boris Karloff, was released in 1932. Along with *Dracula* (1931) and *Frankenstein* (1931), the movie made Universal Pictures very famous in the 1930s.

13

Karloff's makeup is based on the Pharaoh Ramesses III. He spent eight hours a day having it applied. The many layers of cotton glued to his face made it difficult to speak.

The Mummy was a success at the box office. It was especially popular in the **United Kingdom**. The film received mostly positive reviews from critics.

LEGACY

The Mummy has no official **sequels**. But it has been remade many times throughout the years.

There have been film series, comic book **adaptations**, and an animated television series about the mummy.

The film's poster once held the record for the most money paid for a movie poster at an **auction**. It was bought for $453,500.

GLOSSARY

adaptation – a composition, such as literature or music, that is rewritten in a new form.

archeologist – one who studies the remains of people and activities from ancient times.

architect – a person who plans and designs buildings. His or her work is called architecture.

auction – a sale at which goods are sold to the highest bidder.

figure – a well-known or important thing.

mummify – to preserve a dead body in preparation for burial.

pyramid – a triangular structure made of stone used as a royal tomb in ancient Egypt.

sequel – a movie or other work that continues the story begun in a preceding one.

United Kingdom – the united countries of England, Scotland, Wales, and Northern Ireland.

ONLINE RESOURCES

Booklinks
NONFICTION NETWORK
FREE! ONLINE NONFICTION RESOURCES

To learn more about The Mummy, please visit **abdobooklinks.com**. These links are routinely monitored and updated to provide the most current information available.

INDEX

adaptation 19

box office 17

Dracula 12

Egypt 4

film 4, 12, 15, 17, 18, 21

Frankenstein 12

Imhotep 4, 10

Karloff, Boris 12, 15

King Tutankhamun 7

makeup 15

Pharaoh Ramesses III 15

poster 21

Universal Pictures 12